W0254422
This book belongs to
SOAP

To my children, Blake and Ocean – M.H.

To my super girls, Evy and Scarlett – R.F.

First published 2023 by Macmillan Children's Books
an imprint of Pan Macmillan
The Smithson, 6 Briset Street, London EC1M 5NR
EU representative: Macmillan Publishers Ireland Ltd, 1st Floor,
The Liffey Trust Centre, 117-126 Sheriff Street Upper, Dublin 1, D01 YC43

www.panmacmillan.com

ISBN: 978-1-5290-8389-7

1 3 5 7 9 8 6 4 2

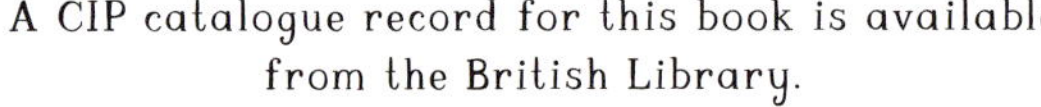

A CIP catalogue record for this book is available
from the British Library.

Printed in China

Marvyn Harrison

Rochelle Falconer

Macmillan Children's Books

Every morning, when we wake up,
we try to be our best selves.

Our daddy likes to help us. He teaches us what we can do to take care of ourselves and other people . . .

I CAN KEEP CLEAN!

It helps me to stay healthy and look my best.

I have a bath.

I brush my teeth.

I wear clean clothes.

I wash my hands, especially after I use the toilet.

Can you sing the alphabet while you wash your hands?

I CAN EAT HEALTHILY!

It makes me feel
full of energy!

I choose healthy snacks.

I drink lots of water.

I like to try different foods.

I eat fruits and vegetables.

Can you name four fruits and vegetables?

I CAN EXERCISE!

It makes me fit and strong.

I practise my football skills.

I dance to music.

Can you show us your best dance move?

I walk to the shops with my daddy.

I can even do cartwheels!

I CAN REST!

It helps me to recharge
for the things I love to do.

I go to bed on time
and get plenty of sleep.

I sit on my
thinking step.

I take a nap
during the day.

I use mindfulness to help me feel calm.

Can you sit in the lotus pose like us?

I CAN EXPRESS MYSELF!

This helps me feel powerful.

I can choose my own clothes.

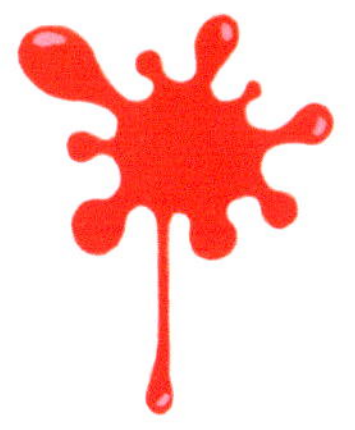

I can paint pictures of my family.

I can do puzzles of African countries by myself.

I can choose a name for my pet.

I CAN SAY NO!

I do it when something doesn't feel good.

Sometimes I don't want to be tickled.

Sometimes I don't want a hug.

Sometimes I don't want more food.

Sometimes I don't like people
touching my hair.
Please don't
touch my hair.

I CAN TALK ABOUT FEELINGS!

They are part
of who I am.

When I am sad,
I talk to my daddy.

Who do you tell
when you are sad?

I ask my friends
if they are OK.

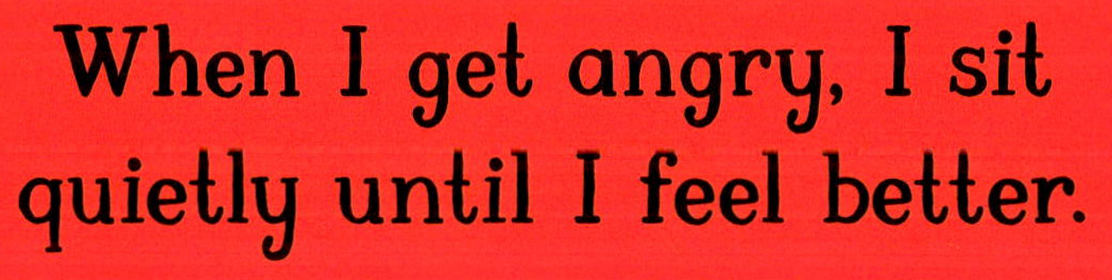

When I get angry, I sit
quietly until I feel better.

When I am happy, I share
my joy with other people!

It makes me feel good to help other people.

I help my daddy clean up.

I pick up litter on the street.

I call my grandparents.

I give away my old clothes and toys.

Thank you, Daddy, for teaching us to be the very best we can be.
Can you KEEP CLEAN, BE KIND and EXPRESS YOURSELF too?
STORMZY
Say it with us LOUDLY . . .

NOTES FOR PARENTS AND CARERS

Marvyn Harrison

Each and every child is special, and it is important that we tell them so every day.

The way I do this with my children is to stand in front of a mirror and shout loudly all the best things about ourselves. We call this 'mirror talk' or 'affirmations' and they are an important part of our self-care routine.

The statements in this book can be read as affirmations, too - why not try them with your own child? Just make sure they say the words LOUDLY and have a big smile on their face! Affirmations help a child to have a strong and healthy mind for when they grow up.

Here are some suggestions to get you started . . .

There are so many things we can all do to show the world how amazing and helpful we are.

Can you try doing these things, too?

I grow plants in my garden.
I am kind to animals.
I learn to say hello in my friends' languages.
As-salamu alaykum
Ni hao
Bonjour
Hola
I try my best when things are difficult.
I give to people who have less than me.

YES

I

CAN!

Say the affirmations in front of a mirror.
This allows your child to see themselves while together you celebrate all of their best parts.

Encourage your child to look at their reflection.
For many children, eye contact is great for developing their confidence.

Say the affirmations loudly.
This helps your child to remember just how amazing they are!

Make it fun!
Playful poses and funny voices can really help your child to stay focused throughout.

Let your child choose their own affirmations.
This makes the activity much more personal and reflects how they feel in the moment.

You might like to end with a hug.
This can help your child to feel safe and loved.

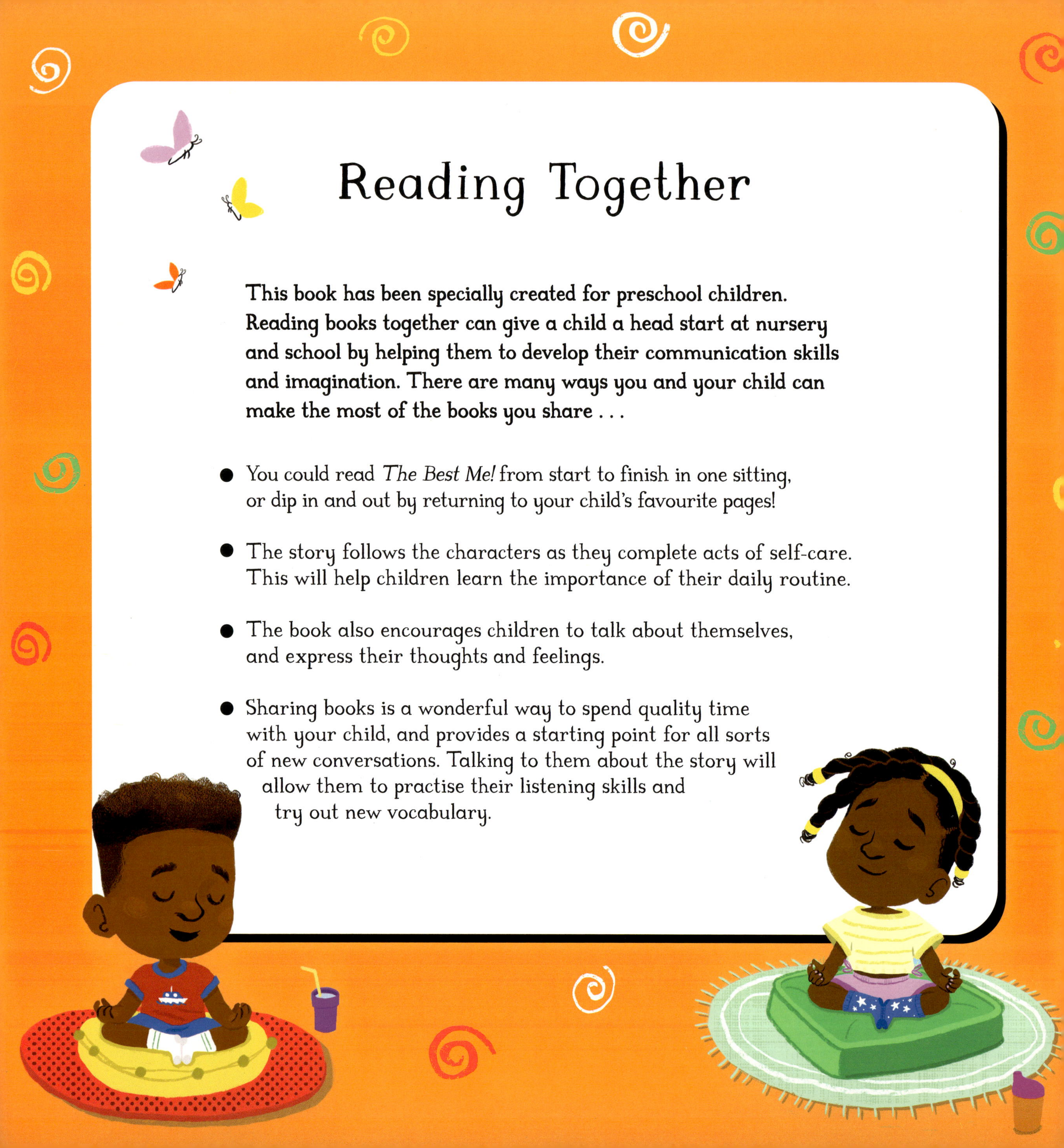

Reading Together

This book has been specially created for preschool children. Reading books together can give a child a head start at nursery and school by helping them to develop their communication skills and imagination. There are many ways you and your child can make the most of the books you share . . .

- You could read *The Best Me!* from start to finish in one sitting, or dip in and out by returning to your child's favourite pages!
- The story follows the characters as they complete acts of self-care. This will help children learn the importance of their daily routine.
- The book also encourages children to talk about themselves, and express their thoughts and feelings.
- Sharing books is a wonderful way to spend quality time with your child, and provides a starting point for all sorts of new conversations. Talking to them about the story will allow them to practise their listening skills and try out new vocabulary.

When you read this book together, you could talk to your child about . . .

. . . the activities they do in a typical day. **What happens in your child's daily routine? Do they eat breakfast and choose their own clothes, too?** Which acts of self-care do they enjoy most and why? Are there any that they've learned to do all on their own?

. . . their feelings after doing different activities, like brushing their teeth or playing outside. **Ask your child how they feel after having a bath.** Talk about how looking after your body can help you look after your mind.

. . . the words the characters use to talk about themselves. Why is it important to be kind? **Which positive words would your child use to describe themselves?** How would they describe the people around them?

. . . things to spot. Try using the book to play a game of I-spy. How many times can your child spot Stormzy the dog? **Choose different things for your child to find**. Then see if they can find some things for you to spot too!